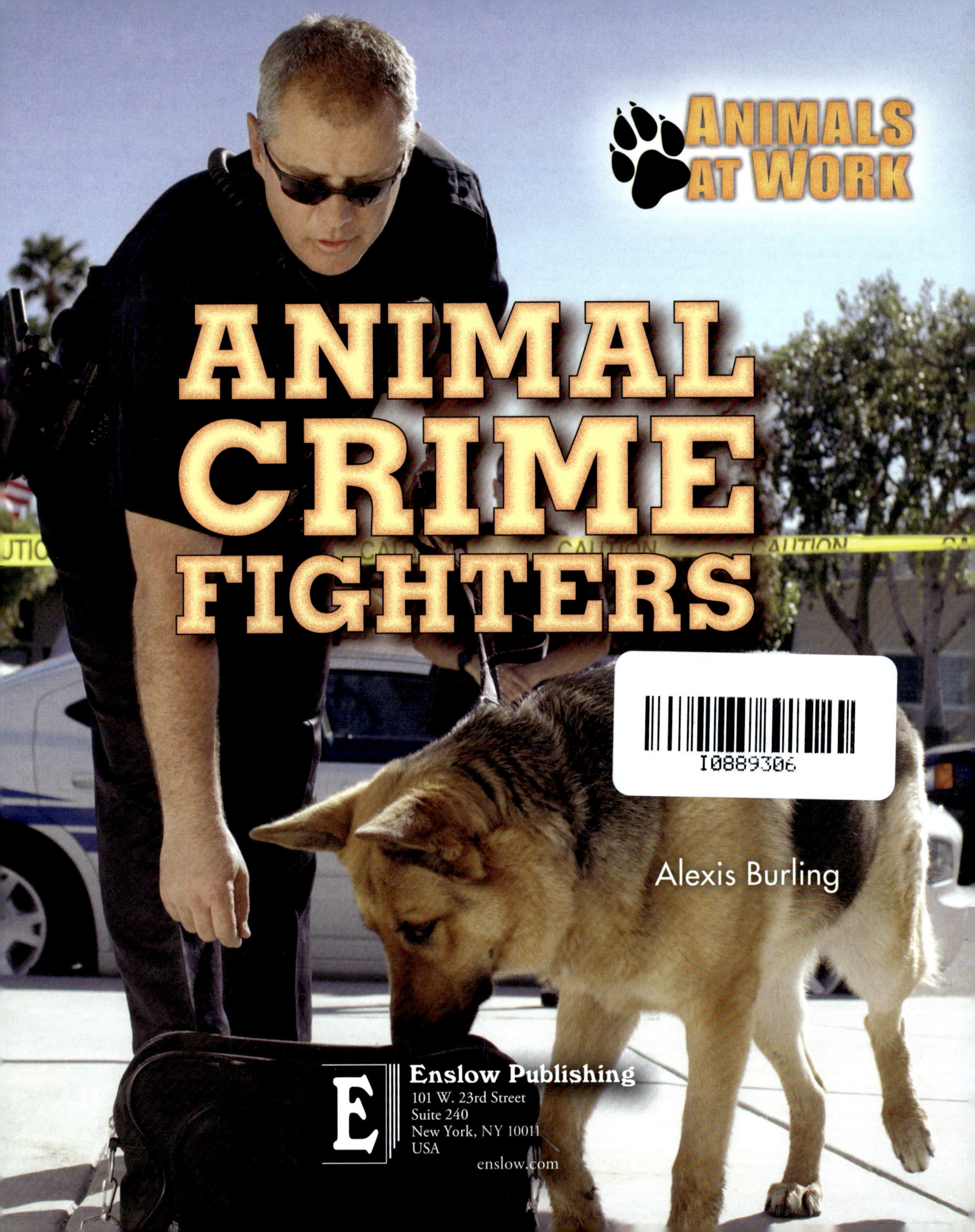

ANIMALS AT WORK

ANIMAL CRIME FIGHTERS

Alexis Burling

Enslow Publishing
101 W. 23rd Street
Suite 240
New York, NY 10011
USA
enslow.com

Words to Know

aggressive Mean; ready to fight or attack.

analyzing Studying something in order to learn about it.

arson Setting fire to a building or piece of property on purpose.

detection The act of discovering something or where something is.

illegal Against the law.

investigators People who try to learn the facts about an event to discover why or how it happened.

mucus A gooey, slippery substance.

obedient Willing to follow rules or do what someone tells you to do.

olfactory Connected to the sense of smell.

threatening When something might cause harm to someone or something.

CONTENTS

Introduction

In 1986, a member of the Connecticut State Police force made history. She was the first female in the world to use her nose to figure out how a fire got started. But she wasn't a *human* female. Mattie was a black Labrador retriever.

When she was one year old, Mattie started her training as an arson-detection dog. Arson is when people start dangerous fires on purpose. It is against the law.

Because of their excellent sense of smell, dogs like Mattie are trained to work on arson cases. They sniff the ground and search for fire-starting ingredients like gasoline. Mattie served on the Connecticut State Police force for six years. She helped solve nearly four hundred arson-related crimes! Her nose led to the arrest of many criminals.

A dog puts her snout to the ground to help solve an arson case in Los Angeles.

True Tests

During training, Mattie took many tests. In one, she correctly sniffed gasoline on one shoe out of a group of eighteen! She got so excited that she peed on the carpet.

"She set a standard that was very high," retired trooper first class Douglas Lancelot told the *Hartford Courant*, a newspaper in Connecticut.

Before there were arson-detection dogs, fire investigators used their eyes to find clues. The process took a long time and had lots of errors. But Mattie solved that problem. Her nose was almost always right, Lancelot said.

Fact

In order to pass her training course, Mattie had to identify seventeen types of chemicals used to start fires.

Mattie's success led to the creation of other doggie arson-detection units. Programs are now in place in other parts of the United States. There are also some in Canada, the Netherlands, and Australia.

It can be hard to find evidence after a fire!

Mattie is not the only courageous critter fighting crime around the world. There are other dogs, horses, cats, and even monkeys that solve crimes! Keep reading to find out more about these animals at work.

1

Super Sniffers

Dogs are the most common animals used to fight crime. Why? Like Mattie, most have a terrific sense of smell. According to scientists, some dogs' noses are so sharp that they can sniff out one rotten apple out of two million barrels of the fruit!

To understand why dogs' noses work so much better than ours do, let's start by learning how our own sense of smell works. Humans have between five and six million olfactory, or smell, receptors in our bodies. Olfactory receptors are the parts of our nose that allow us to smell many kinds of odors. We breathe in air, which goes to our lungs. Along the way, the air passes

Fact

The part of a dog's brain that is used for analyzing smells is forty times larger than the same area in a human.

Dogs have the ability to take in air and breathe it out at the same time.

through an area of the nose that helps us smell different scents.

Dogs also breathe air into and out of their lungs. But the way they smell is more complicated. Dogs have up to three hundred million olfactory receptors in their snouts! They also have a small nook in the back of their nose that humans do not have. When a dog breathes in, about 12 percent of the

Nifty Noses

Why are dogs' noses always wet? The mucus on a dog's nose helps it smell by capturing scent particles.

air goes to that special place. This is where smells are examined.

Because of this area, dogs have a more detailed sense of smell than humans do. Some scientists say it is one thousand to ten thousand times stronger! This comes in handy when fighting crimes. Police dogs can track missing people and find lost objects because of their amazing noses.

2

Trusted Trainers

Do you have a pet at home? If so, think about why you are so close. It probably has something to do with the tasty treats you give your pet. But people and their pets also bond because they trust each other. The same is true for police dogs and their trainers.

Each police dog is assigned to its own police officer. This helps the dog become comfortable around humans. More importantly, it teaches the dog how to trust one person above everyone else. A police dog-and-officer team is called a K-9 unit. "Canine" is another word for dog.

Fact

Anxious, shy, or aggressive pups are not picked for crime-fighting jobs because their personalities could put them or their officer in danger.

Police officer Michelle Cole and her canine partner stick together to fight crime.

Most police dogs live with their officers. The officers are also the dogs' trainers. At home, there is plenty of time for goofing around. But to become police dogs, puppies must go through a challenging training process before they are allowed to work.

First, there is basic training. The puppies learn how to follow commands. They are taught not to bite, chew, bark, jump, or run away. In order to get to the next round, they have to pass tests where they can show they know how to follow directions.

Then the dogs are taught special skills. Some dogs learn how to sniff out bombs or drugs. Others learn about search and rescue to help find missing people or things. All police dogs are trained using loud noises and surprises to prepare them for a real day on the job.

Best in Show

Police departments use certain dog breeds for K-9 teams. Bloodhounds and Labrador retrievers are the most common dogs used in detection work or search-and-rescue jobs.

K-9 training is tough! Dogs must know how to sit, stay, and heel.

K-9 training is also about staying in shape. Police work is tiring! The dogs need to be able to run up the stairs or leap over a wall quickly and easily.

3

Dedicated Detectives

Once a police dog finishes its training and passes its tests, it is time to go out on the job. But the hard part is not over. With long shifts and lots of running around, police dogs do as much work as their human partners.

K-9 dogs ride in the police car on each shift. They sit in a part of the car away from where criminals are kept. The dogs are trained to tackle someone who seems threatening. Sometimes they chase bad people who try to escape.

Most police dogs are also cross-trained. This means they know how to do more than one job. Some dogs are taught to find weapons, money, or drugs hidden at crime scenes.

Fact

It would take human police officers ten times as long to search the same area as a dog—and they'd still never find everything a police dog can uncover.

Police dogs sit in the back seat when they go on patrol.

Drug-sniffing pooches are also used at border control checkpoints and in airports.

When a police dog finds a strange object where it is not supposed to be, the dog gives its handler an alert signal. Drug-sniffing dogs use a signal when they find something. They paw at the ground.

Other police dogs learn how to search for bombs. Bomb-sniffing dogs cannot paw at the ground. Too much

A security officer leads a bomb-sniffing dog at an airport in Israel.

Beagle Brigade

The US Department of Agriculture uses the Beagle Brigade, a group of beagles, in airports to sniff out produce that isn't allowed in the country. If the dogs smell illegal fruits or vegetables, they sit by the suitcase until its owner is caught.

digging could cause an explosion! Instead, the dogs use a different kind of alert. They sit and point their nose toward the area where a bomb might be.

Police work is dangerous. But K-9 units are careful. The best breeds for this type of work are German shepherds and Belgian Malinois.

4

Search and Rescue

Pooches on patrol have mighty fine noses. In addition to finding drugs or bombs, they also look for people. These brave and courageous dogs search for hikers lost in the wilderness, earthquake victims, or people hurt in a plane crash.

Search-and-rescue pups are either tracking dogs or air-scenting dogs. Trackers scour an area with their

This search-and-rescue pup sniffs the air for human scent.

Fact

Experts say that one search-and-rescue dog can accomplish the work of twenty to thirty human searchers.

noses to the ground. Air-scenting dogs work with their snouts held high. Each follows human scent. They track perfume, tiny skin particles, or even bits of clothing left behind by the person they are searching for.

Search-and-rescue work is very rewarding. But some police dogs have a dirtier job. Instead of looking for someone alive, they try to find someone—or the body parts of someone—who has been killed. They also sniff out buried weapons or murderers on the run. Some dogs can even find a dead person underwater!

Top-Notch Searchers

In addition to a superior sniffer, dogs have outstanding hearing and night vision. Some of the best breeds for search-and-rescue work are golden retrievers, bearded collies, and Bernese mountain dogs.

Sagus, a German Shepherd police dog, is photographed wearing a bulletproof vest.

In most police work, it is possible that a bad person with a gun could be hidden behind a corner. For that reason, many police dogs wear bulletproof vests while on the job. It keeps them safe—and it makes them look tough, too! Some search-and-rescue dogs even wear goggles to protect their eyes from smoke or harmful chemicals.

5

Towering Transport

By now you have learned all about pups used in police work. But dogs are not the only crime-fighting animals. Throughout history, horses have played a major role in helping cops get their jobs done. Why? Aside from giraffes, horses are some of the tallest animals around!

Thanks to their large bodies and towering height, horses are used in police departments all over the world. In cities, horses patrol areas where cars are not allowed, such as narrow streets, crowded sidewalks, or parks. A mounted police officer can observe a bigger area than someone just standing on the ground. If a

Fact

Formed on September 7, 1825, the New South Wales Mounted Police Force in Australia is the oldest ongoing mounted unit in the world.

Horses help police officers patrol the streets in Montreal, Canada.

policeman is chasing someone, horses are much faster than a running person.

In rural areas, horses carry police into regions where cars cannot go, such as deep into the wilderness. Just like dogs, horses have a great sense of smell. But they also have another valuable skill: their hearing.

There are ten muscles in a horse's ear compared to three in a human's. These muscles control movement. That is why a horse can turn each ear in a separate direction to listen. It helps them hear where a sound is coming from. They can hear something that happens up to 2.5 miles (4 kilometers) away!

Camels are used for police work in countries like Egypt and Jordan.

Capable Camels

Some countries do not use horses for police work. In Egypt and India, they use camels instead. Camels can carry heavy loads. They can also go a long time without water.

Horses have many jobs on a police force. They carry officers around and keep crowds under control, too. In order to fight crime, horses must listen to orders. They have to be comfortable walking on grass, dirt, concrete, and in water.

6

Crime Fighter Hall of Fame

In the United States, Canada, and many parts of the world, dogs and horses are the best crime fighters in the business. But in some countries, other animals get a chance to show their stuff, too. Here are a few fun examples of animals known for being tough on crime. Welcome to the Animal Crime Fighter Hall of Fame!

Santisuk

Santisuk is a pig-tailed macaque monkey. He was a proud member of the police force in the Yala province of southern Thailand. He went out on patrol every day

The pig-tailed macaque monkey got its name because of its short, squiggly tail.

Larry is another famous cat. He lives in London, England, with the British prime minister.

Take a Bite Out of Crime

McGruff the Crime Dog is not a real dog. He is a cartoon figure that was created in 1979. During the 1980s, McGruff was featured in billboards, TV, radio, and newspaper ads to teach the public about crime and safety.

wearing his own police uniform. Sometimes he helped locals collect coconuts.

Lemon

When he turned two weeks old, Lemon the cat became a police officer in Kyoto, Japan. Sometimes

In 2000, McGruff had his twentieth birthday with second graders in Denver.

Eagles get rid of drones by snatching them out of the sky with their feet.

he helps the cops sniff out crime scenes. But mostly he stays at the station to keep the other officers—and prisoners—calm.

The Dutch Flying Squad

There are flying robots called drones. Some drones fly too close to airports. In the Netherlands, a Dutch police department started the first eagle-training program. These eagles knock the drones out of the sky.

LEARN MORE

Books

Boothroyd, Jennifer. *Hero Law Enforcement Dogs*. Minneapolis, MN: Lerner Books, 2017.

Quattlebaum, Mary. *Hero Dogs*. Washington, DC: National Geographic Society, 2017.

Shotz, Jennifer Lee. *Hero: Hurricane Rescue*. New York, NY: HarperCollins, 2017.

Websites

ASPCA

https://www.aspca.org

The American Society for the Prevention of Cruelty to Animals is a national group that works to prevent animal abuse.

The Beagle Brigade

https://www.cbp.gov/border-security/protecting-agriculture/agriculture-canine

Find out more about the US Department of Agriculture's canine unit, which makes a vital contribution to the country's national security.

National Police Dogs Foundation

https://nationalpolicedogfoundation.org

This foundation promotes education and awareness and raises money for the training and ongoing care for active and retired police dogs.

INDEX

Published in 2019 by Enslow Publishing, LLC.
101 W. 23rd Street, Suite 240, New York, NY 10011

Library of Congress Cataloging-in-Publication Data

Names: Burling, Alexis, author.
Title: Animal crime fighters / Alexis Burling.
Description: New York : Enslow Publishing, [2019] | Series: Animals at work | Audience: Grade 3-6. | Includes bibliographical references and index.
Identifiers: LCCN 2017051694| ISBN 9780766096158 (library bound) | ISBN 9780766096165 (pbk.) | ISBN 9780766096172 (6 pack)
Subjects: LCSH: Police dogs—Juvenile literature.
Classification: LCC HV8025 .B787 2018 | DDC 363.28—dc23
LC record available at https://lccn.loc.gov/2017051694

Printed in the United States of America

To Our Readers: We have done our best to make sure all website addresses in this book were active and appropriate when we went to press. However, the author and the publisher have no control over and assume no liability for the material available on those websites or on any websites they may link to. Any comments or suggestions can be sent by e-mail to customerservice@enslow.com.

Photo Credits: Cover, p. 1 sirtravelalot/Shutterstock.com; p. 5 Brian Vander Brug/Los Angeles Times/Getty Images; p. 7 Ron Frank/Shutterstock.com; p. 9 Lorenzo Patoia/Shutterstock.com; p. 12 Portland Press Herald/Getty Images; p. 14 Nicky Rhodes/Shutterstock.com; p. 16 Radius Images/Alamy Stock Photo; p. 17 Jack Guez/AFP/Getty Images; p. 19 JeanPhilippe Babu/Shutterstock.com; p. 21 Mel Melcon/Los Angeles Times/Getty Images; p. 23 meunierd/Shutterstock.com; p. 24 Delpixel/Shutterstock.com; p. 27 shene/Moment Open/Getty Images; p. 28 Carl Court/AFP/Getty Images; p. 29 Dave Buresh/Denver Post/Getty Images; p. 30 Igor Kovalenko/Shutterstock.com.